## THIS BOOK BELONGS TO . . .

D1227606

Write your name and decorate your dressing room
door however you want so your fellow Superstars
will know who's in the house!

# BuzzPop

An imprint of Little Bee Books
New York, NY
Copyright © 2021 by WWE

Shutterstock: 1 full PixelSquid360; 6 full queezz; 7 full sapol; 8, 10, 75 Milan M; 14 Piotr Urakau; 12, 44, 46, 75, 80 wanpatsorn; 25 full sapol; 25 bottom viledevil; 26-27 full Sergey Mastepanov; halftone throughout Miloje; 38 full marivlada; 42-43 full antart; 40, 45, 46 Hurst Photo; 52 full sokolovski; 53, 54 full Alexey Pushkin; dithering throughout johnjohnson; 72-73 Vozzy Public Domain; grid paper throughout; gold seal 92; notebook paper throughout Pexel; 50-51 Envato: 1 full PixelSquid360; 89 full markusgann; 25 bottom Galyna_Andrushko; 68-69 full IciakPhotos

BuzzPop and associated colophon are trademarks of Little Bee Books.
Manufactured in China TPL 1120

First Edition

10 9 8 7 6 5 4 3 2 1

For more information about special discounts on bulk purchases, please contact Little Bee Books at sales@littlebeebooks.com.

ISBN 978-1-4998-1175-9

buzzpopbooks.com

# YOU'RE A SUPERSTAR!

## GUIDED ACTIVITIES TO UNLOCK YOUR STAR POWER!

# IT'S GO TIME!

## THERE'S NO TURNING BACK NOW, CHAMP!

BuzzPop

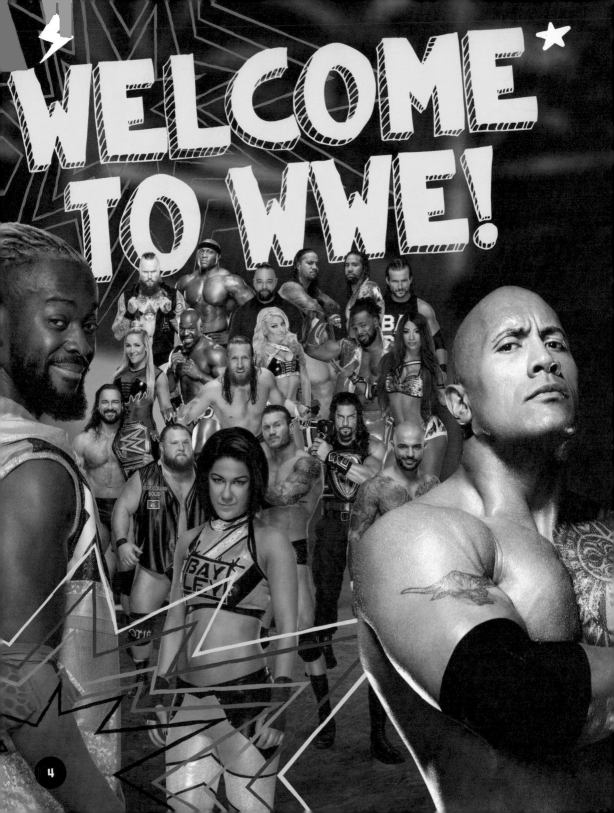

# WELCOME* TO WWE!

# YOUR FELLOW SUPERSTARS ARE HERE TO SHOW YOU THE ROPES.

# HEY THERE, SUPERSTAR!

If your hopes and dreams are to one day step into a WWE ring, you've gotta know exactly what it takes to become a WWE Superstar.

Have you written your theme song? Have you designed a championship-level exercise routine? Have you imagined what it will take to climb the ladder to grab the Money in the Bank briefcase? To be the best WWE Superstar you can be, you'll need to make sure you've thought about everything from your very first match to your induction into the WWE Hall of Fame!

Luckily, you've come to the right place. This book is filled with activities, projects, and guides to help you along the way. And the best part? Your favorite WWE Superstars are here to cheer you on!

So, what are you waiting for? The journey to becoming a WWE Superstar starts right here.

# NAME THAT SUPERSTAR!

Use this space to introduce your Superstar self to the WWE Universe! Pick your Superstar name and design your Superstar logo so fans can get to know exactly who you are.

NOTE: Remember, this is your logo. Incorporate your favorite colors, designs, and interests as much as you want!

# WHO ARE YOU?

Your future fans are going to want to know as much as they can about your absolute awesomeness. Start with this survey and show 'em what you're made of!

Real Name _____

Birthday _____

Hometown _____

Zodiac Sign _____

Best Friend _____

Pets _____

Favorite TV Show _____

Favorite Movie _____

Favorite Band _____

Favorite Song _____

Favorite WWE Superstar _____

Favorite Food _____

Favorite Class _____

Favorite Sport _____

Least Favorite TV Show _____

Least Favorite Movie _____

Least Favorite Band _____

Least Favorite Song _____

Least Favorite WWE Superstar _____

Least Favorite Food _____

Least Favorite Class _____

Least Favorite Sport _____

Why do you want to be a WWE Superstar?

_____

_____

_____

_____

_____

_____

_____

_____

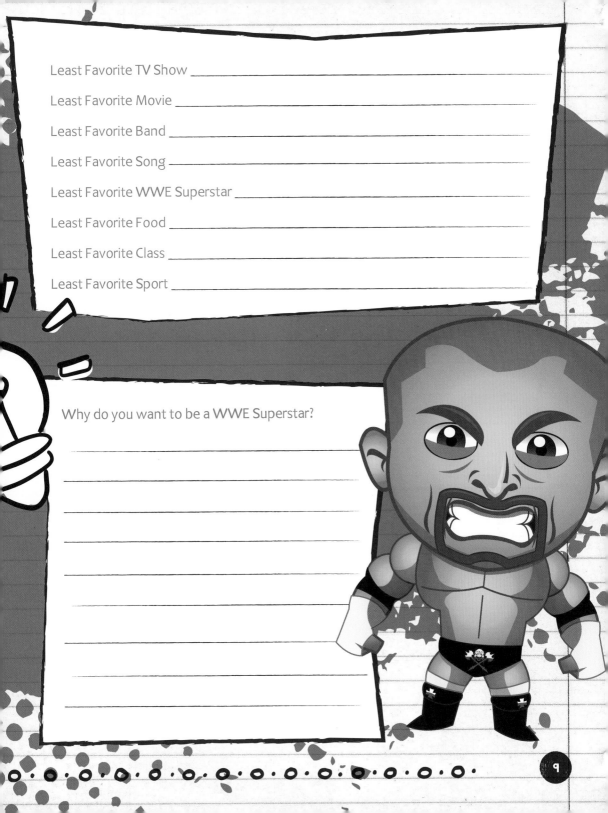

What's the most challenging thing you've ever had to do?

_____
_____
_____
_____

What achievement are you most proud of?

_____
_____
_____
_____

What are you the absolute best at?

_____
_____
_____
_____

What's something in your life that you could use some help with?

_____

_____

_____

_____

What's one secret about you that no one knows?

_____

_____

_____

_____

Who else in your house loves WWE as much as you do?

_____

_____

_____

# YOU'VE GOT THE MIC!

Now, imagine you've got the chance to interview any WWE Superstar you want. Who would it be, and what would you ask them? Have a friend or family member play the Superstar to give you the answers!

My interview with: _____
(Superstar's name here)

By: _____
(your name here)

Question 1: Who is your favorite Superstar?

Answer: _____

Question 2: Who is your least favorite Superstar?

Answer: _____

Question 3: Where is the coolest place you've ever been?

Answer: _____

Question 4: What is your proudest WWE moment?

Answer: _____

Question 5: What is one thing you're still working
to accomplish in WWE?

Answer: _____

Question 6: What advice do you have for a future
WWE Superstar? (Me!)

Answer: _____

_____

_____

_____

# YOU'RE A-MAZE-ING!

Being a WWE Superstar means overcoming obstacles. Can you find your way through WWE Headquarters without getting stuck, stopped, or (gulp!) slammed?

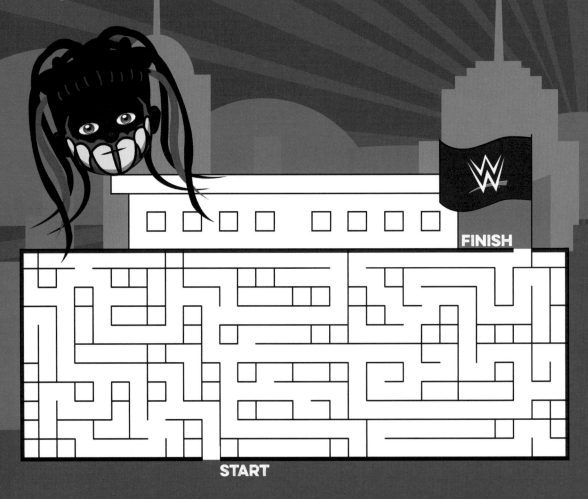

FINISH

START

Answer key on pages 93–95

# DRESS FOR SUCCESS

To be a WWE Superstar, you've gotta look the part. Design yourself as the best-looking Superstar in the business and decorate your gear. Then cut out and model your ultimate outfit!

Cut around the dotted lines with the help of an adult.

18

# WAIT A MINUTE...

Something's not right! Use your keen eye to spot the 5 differences between the two photos below. Circle them all and don't tap out!

Answer key on pages 93–95

# GEAR UP!

The best way to spot your fans in the crowd is to make sure they're sporting the sweetest swag on the planet. Design your own Superstar stuff for them to show off their support for you!

# SUPERSTAR IN DISGUISE!

As a top **WWE** Superstar, you might not always want to be in the spotlight. That's what masks are for! Design this blank mask however you want, then cut it out, and slip it on to fool even your most fanatical followers.

Cut out mask along dotted lines. Punch out holes at the sides and use string to tie mask around your head.

24

# SUPERSTAR FACE-OFF!

Who can be a friend to you on your journey to the top? See if you can guess the identities of these Superstars!

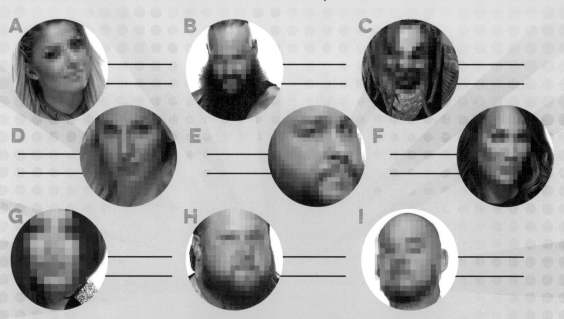

A _____

B _____

C _____

D _____

E _____

F _____

G _____

H _____

I _____

Each of these pics represents something having to do with **WWE**. Can you use your mega-mind muscles to figure out what they are?

1

2 +

3

_____

4 BUCKLE

5 N XT

_____

Answer key on pages 93–95

# WHAT SIGNS CAN YOU SEE?

What do you hope the WWE Universe will say about you?
Write and draw the signs that will keep you going strong.

# DRAW THE WWE CHAMPIONSHIP BELT IN 4 EASY STEPS!

It's only a matter of time before you capture the real WWE Championship. For now, you can practice on a separate sheet of paper with these easy instructions.

**Step 1:** Draw two Ws like this.

**Step 2:** Add some borders.

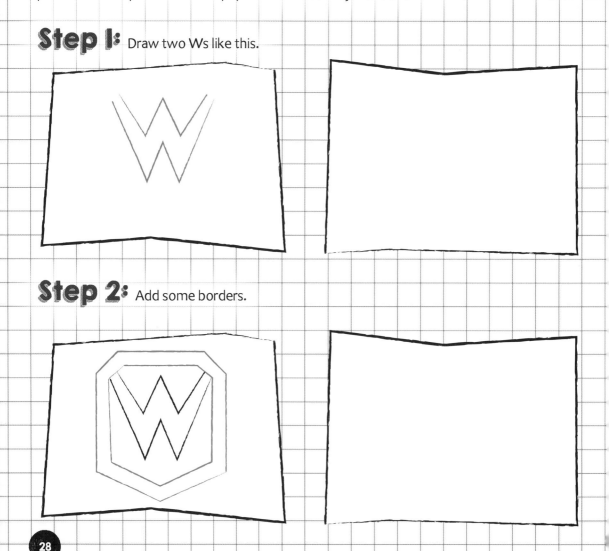

# Step 3: Draw some bold outlines around your Ws.

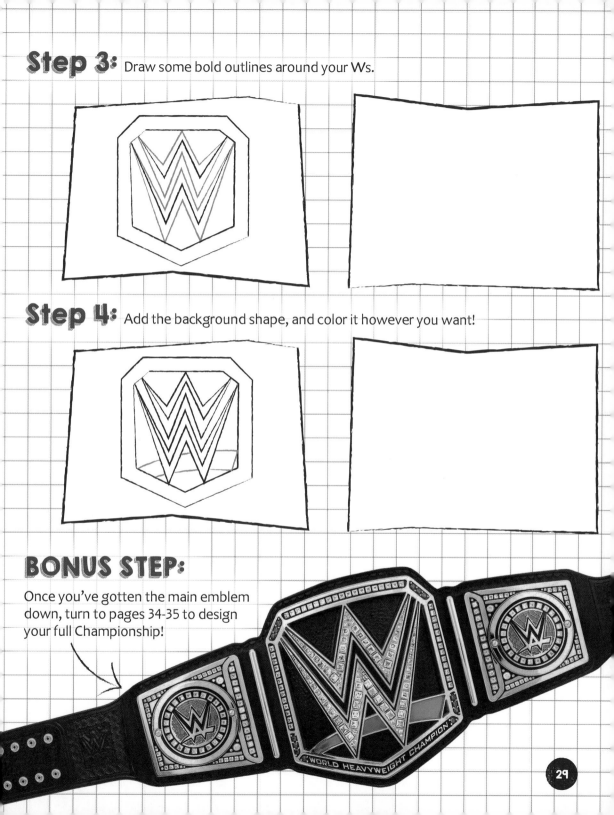

# Step 4: Add the background shape, and color it however you want!

# BONUS STEP:

Once you've gotten the main emblem down, turn to pages 34-35 to design your full Championship!

WORLD HEAVYWEIGHT CHAMPION

# FRUITY FACTS!

Enjoy these delicious treats that'll give you endless energy while you chase the championship!

## APPLES
Want a stylin' Superstar 'do? The vitamins in an apple a day will stimulate your hair to grow and grow!

## BANANAS
Packed with potassium, bananas will help prevent muscle cramps and allow you to bend, dodge, and pivot with ease!

## WATERMELONS
The vitamin A in watermelon can help power your peepers to see better at night! Perfect for navigating dark entrances like Undertaker's or The Fiend's!

## ORANGES
Eating these will strengthen your skeleton with calcium, so you can toughen up everything from your toes to your teeth!

## GRAPES
Even though they're tiny, grapes have huge benefits— like helping your eyesight watch out for challengers!

# VIGOROUS VEGGIES!

Veggies get a bad rap. Here's why they're perfect for your journey to the title.

### BROCCOLI

The vitamin C in broccoli can help your body heal and recover from tough training sessions!

### CARROTS

They're great for tooth and gum health, which you'll need for that Superstar smile!

### BELL PEPPERS

Because they're high in fiber, they'll keep your body running smoothly all match long. Plus, look at those awesome colors!

### GREEN BEANS

If you don't want to tire out, eat some of these—their iron content will help your body make red blood cells to help transport oxygen more effectively.

### CELERY

Superstars do a lot of sweating, which is why the sodium in celery is perfect for keeping your body cool.

# BE A SOCIAL SUPERSTAR!

Fans from all over the world will want to see what a top Superstar like you is up to! Let them follow along by completing these practice profiles where you can talk, post, and tell everyone what's up!

SCREEN NAME

CITY/STATE

BIO

PHOTOS

POSTS

**SCREEN NAME**

**CITY/STATE**

**POSTS**

**BIO**

**PHOTOS**

**SCREEN NAME**

**CITY/STATE**

**BIO**

**PHOTOS**

**POSTS**

Make sure to always get an
adult's permission before
going online or checking out
any social networking site!

33

# CREATE YOUR CUSTOM CHAMPIONSHIP!

Top Superstars have been customizing their Championship belts forever. And since you're on the road to earning your own, you can get started by designing it however you want! Add color. Add your name. Add . . . whatever you want!

34

# COPY AND COLOR

Use these guidance grids to copy the Superstar pictures provided. When you're all sharing a locker room together, they'll make awesome birthday presents for your fellow wrestlers!

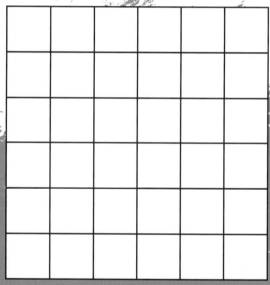

# READY, SET, GOAL!

Whether you're a rockin' rookie or a victorious veteran, every Superstar needs to set goals. If you pick one goal each month that will help you improve yourself, you'll be shining bright all year long. Get started now!

## MONTH:

## WHAT IS MY GOAL FOR THIS MONTH?

## HOW CAN I ACHIEVE THAT GOAL?

## WHAT CHALLENGES MIGHT I FACE?

## WHO CAN I ASK FOR HELP?

BEFORE YOU START! Copy this template twelve times—you can ask for help using a copier, write it in a journal or notebook, or draw it with spaghetti on your dinner plate*—so you can use it for the rest of the year!

*Just make sure not to eat your goals!

# THE ULTIMATE FUTURE WWE SUPERSTAR QUIZ!

Being a WWE Superstar isn't just about winning in the ring. It's about smarts, confidence, and respect. Show your respect for the WWE and your confidence in your smarts by answering the following questions!

1) Who is Finn Bálor's alter ego?

a. The Fiend

b. The Big Red Monster

c. The Viper

d. The Demon King

2) Fill in the blank for the name of this exciting WWE stipulation match: "_____ in the Bank."

a. Sofa cushions

b. Lunch box

c. Money

d. Candy

3) After nine years away, I made my comeback in the 2020 Royal Rumble. Who am I?

a. The Rock

b. John Cena

c. Edge

d. Ric Flair

4) Before being defeated by Brock Lesnar, how many wins were part of Undertaker's undefeated *WrestleMania* streak?

a. 15

b. 21

c. 24

d. 31

5) What is Becky Lynch's hometown?

a. Limerick, Ireland

b. Dublin, Ireland

c. Galway, Ireland

d. Longford, Ireland

6) Which of these Superstars had an undefeated streak that lasted 914 days?

a. Charlotte Flair

b. Asuka

c. Shinsuke Nakamura

d. Finn Bálor

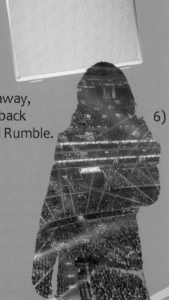

7) Which of the following is NOT one of Bray Wyatt's friends in the Firefly Funhouse?

   a. Ramblin' Rabbit

   b. The Boss

   c. Mercy the Buzzard

   d. Hopkins the Frog

8) Which WWE Superstar uses a move known as the Claymore Kick?

   a. Ricochet

   b. Drew McIntyre

   c. Otis

   d. A.J. Styles

9) How many *WrestleManias* have there been so far?

   a. 30

   b. 34

   c. 36

   d. 40

## HOW'D YOU DO?

All 9 correct – You're unstoppable!

7–8 correct – You've got what it takes!

4–6 correct – Keep practicing!

1–3 correct – Don't give up!

0 correct – Lots of room for improvement!

Answer key on pages 93–95

# CHAMPIONSHIP CHASE!

Team building is important! If you can make it through this tangled, mangled mess, you'll help one of your future Superstar friends earn Championship gold on the other side. (That means they'll owe you one down the road!)

## STEP 1.

Choose your Superstar.

## STEP 2.

Carefully follow his or her path all the way to the Championship at the end.

## STEP 3.

Celebrate with your Superstar pal! That was tricky!

Answer key on
pages 93–95

# CUSTOMIZE YOUR CASE!

Just imagine how it will feel to win your first (but not last!) Money in the Bank Ladder Match. You're worth it! Before you cash it in, decorate it like a real WWE Superstar and cut it out!

Cut around the dotted lines.

Cut around the dotted lines with the help of an adult.

# LET'S WRITE LYRICS

If you want to make a huge impact as a WWE Superstar, you'll need to let everyone know what you're about as soon as you walk through the curtain. W better way to do that than with your own totally unique, customized theme s

Fill in the blanks correctly, then start practicing!

## VERSE 1

Oh, it's me, _____!
(Superstar's name here)

I'm the best _____ there ever will be!
(noun)

I can _____ better than anyone else!
(verb)

I'm always ready for _____ opponents!
(adjective)

## VERSE 2

Everyone is cheering for me, _____!
(Superstar's name here)

I can hear their _____ voices!
(adjective)

They sound so _____ to see me!
(adjective)

I'm the best _____ they've ever seen!
(noun)

## VERSE 3

I'm gonna win my match by _____ing!
(verb)

My opponent can't defeat my _____!
(noun)

I'm ready to earn that Championship!

# SUPERSTAR EYE SPY!

Build your confidence by looking these Superstars in the eyes and trying to guess who's standing in your way!

Write the correct letter in the box of the matching Superstar.

A. SASHA BANKS
B. BECKY LYNCH
C. SETH ROLLINS
D. KOFI KINGSTON
E. THE FIEND
F. JOHN CENA
G. DREW MCINTYRE
H. ASUKA
I. JEFF HARDY
J. DOLPH ZIGGLER
K. ALEXA BLISS
L. SHEAMUS

Answer key on pages 93-95

49

# WHAT KIND OF SUPERSTAR ARE YOU?

Are you a hulking heavyweight? Are you a hip highflyer? Are you a tremendous teammate? Take this quiz to figure out which Superstar role suits you best!

1) Where would you rather go on vacation?

a.     b.     c.

2) What would you rather study in school?

a.     b.     c.

3) What gives you the most energy?

a.     b.     c.

4) If you could be one animal for a day, what would you be?

a.     b.     c.

5) What's your biggest strength?

a.

b.

c.

6) How do you like to help?

a.

b.

c.

7) Which WWE Superstar(s) would you want to train you?

a.

b.

c.

## NOW! LOOK AT ALL YOUR ANSWERS, AND SEE WHAT KIND OF SUPERSTAR YOU'D BE:

Mostly As – You're a heavy-duty heavyweight who can overcome any obstacle in your way as you chase the WWE Championship!

Mostly Bs – You're a high-flying phenom who's fearless and brave!

Mostly Cs – You're a loyal tag team partner who would do anything for your friends and family.

# CHAMPIONSHIP FITNESS

Fitness is fun and a huge part of being a WWE Superstar. What steps can you take to set your fitness goals? Talk with a family member about the best exercises for you and use the following suggestions to get started!

## PACE YOURSELF AND DON'T RUSH

It's always better to have an adult demonstrate an exercise and to do it right rather than fast. Agree on a time limit so that you don't overdo it. Work hard but always work safe!

TODAY I WILL DO_____JUMPING JACKS.

TODAY I WILL DO_____ARM CURLS.

TODAY I WILL DO_____PUSH-UPS.

TODAY I WILL WALK OR RUN_____LAPS.

# SUPERSTAR MEMORY MATCH

Remembering your opponent's strengths and weaknesses is a key part of becoming a WWE Superstar. Cut out these squares and see the instructions on how to play on page 55!

# HERE'S HOW YOU CAN TRAIN YOUR BRAIN TO STAY STRONG!

## STEP 1:

Carefully cut out all of these squares.

## STEP 2:

Flip them over and shuffle them around.

## STEP 3:

Pick them up two at a time and try to get a matching pair. If you don't, place them back in their original spots, and try to remember where they are for next time!

## STEP 4:

See how many matching pairs you can pick up in a row!

# SCRAMBLED SUPERSTARS

Uh-oh! Looks like the names of these 10 WWE Superstars went through the washing machine! Can you sort out the letters and spell them correctly?

## 1) JET SLAYS

This is _____

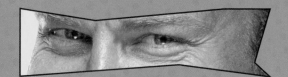

## 2) HOBBY BLAY LES

This is _____

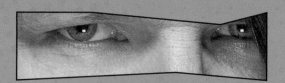

## 3) PREZ HOGG DILL

This is _____

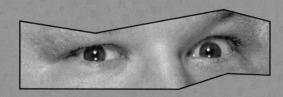

## 4) TIOS

This is _____

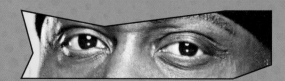

## 5) SHRINE TOLLS

This is _____

## 6) CAROL TETH

This is _____

## 7) DYNATRON OR

This is _____

## 8) TOY RIB RUT

This is _____

## 9) OARSMEN RING

This is _____

## 10) WIRED CRY MENT

This is _____

Answer key on pages 93–95

# LEGIT BOSS FOR A DAY

Every WWE Superstar imagines what it would be like to be in charge of WWE for a day! What sorts of silly rules and stipulations would you apply? Write them below, then design the inside of your brand-new office. (Don't forget the slushy machine and waterslide!)

**IF I WERE IN CHARGE, I WOULD...**

_____      _____

_____      _____

_____      _____

_____      _____

**MY OFFICE**

# CUBE IN A CAGE

Follow these simple instructions to snip, paste, and produce two mini Superstars you can use to practice strategy and master your moves on your way to the Championship.

## STEP 1:

Carefully cut out the pattern along the lines.

## STEP 2:

Fold along the dotted lines, and press those creases so the flaps stay put.

## STEP 3:

Fold the tabs into the inside, add glue to secure them, and get ready to defend your championship!

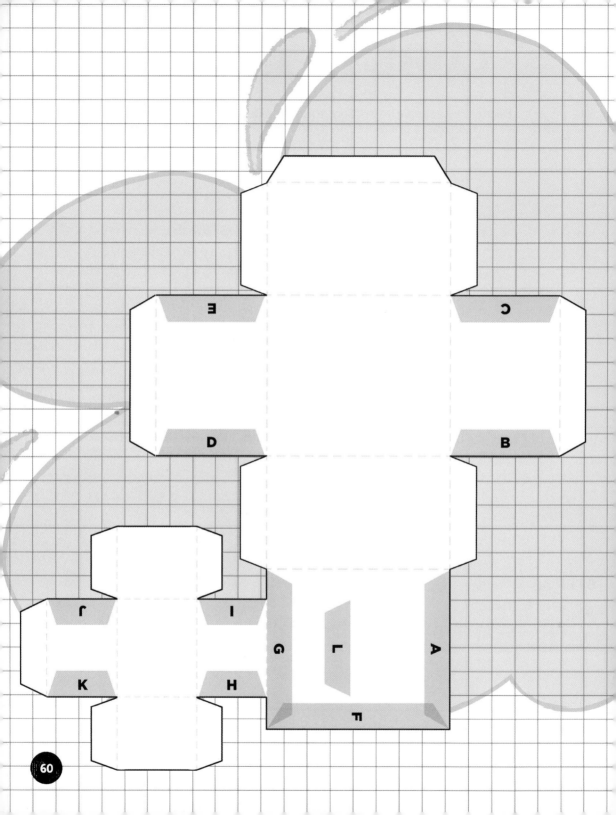

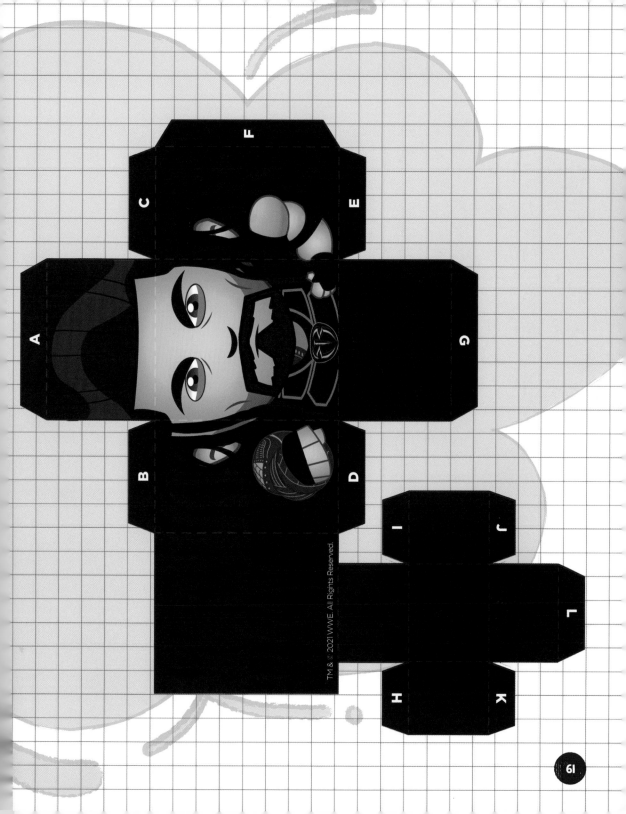

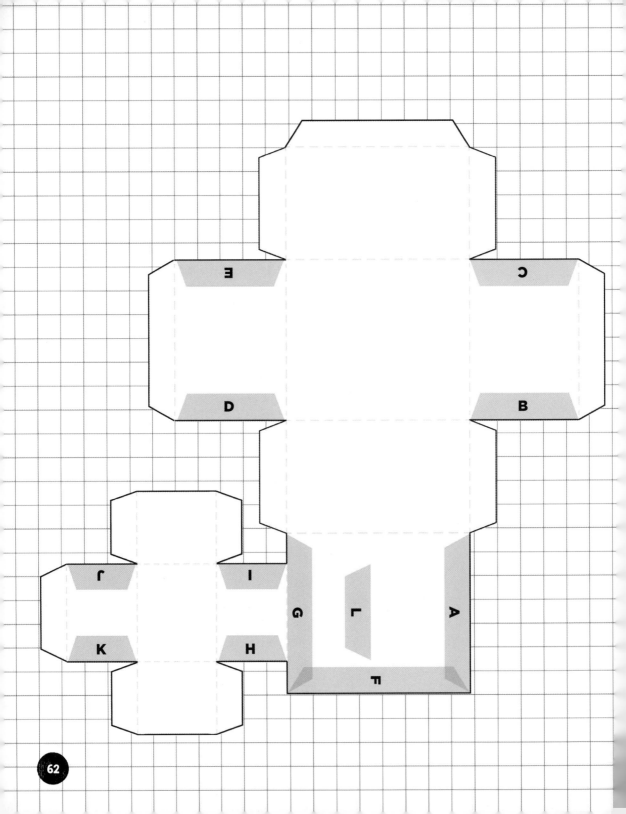

# LEGEND LOOKOUT

Looks like the washing machine got these WWE Legends' names, too. Can you guess who's who and help set things right?

## 1) HONK LA HUG

This is _____

## 2) MOC HAN MA

This is _____

## 3) TWIRLIER ARUM OAT

This is _____

## 4) CHAINSAWS HELM

This is _____

## 5) CORK ETH

This is _____

## 6) NONCULTIVATED OSE ESTS

This is _____

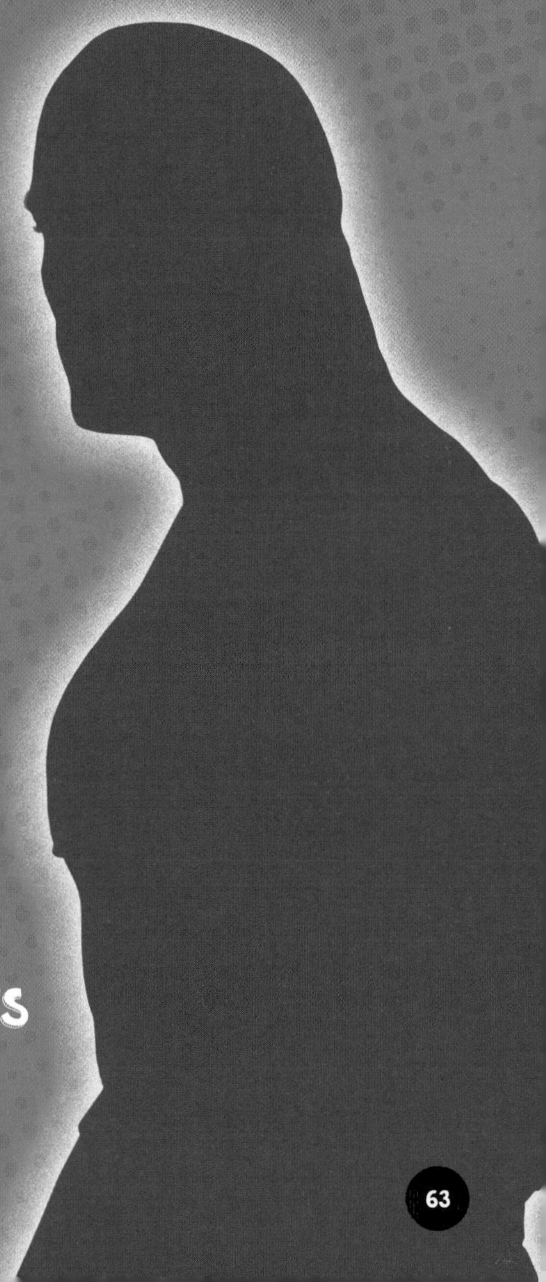

Answer key on pages 93–95

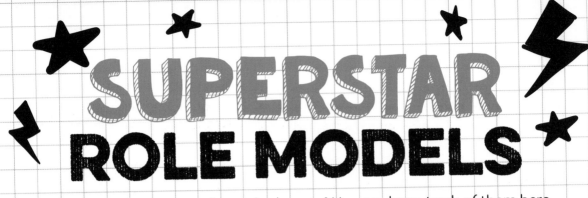

# SUPERSTAR ROLE MODELS

Which WWE Superstars do you look up to? You can keep track of them here, along with why they inspire you to always be your best! Fill in the blanks and draw or add photos of your favorite Superstars in the boxes provided!

## MY FAVORITE WWE SUPERSTAR IS _____

That's because _____
_____
_____

## MY FAVORITE WWE TAG TEAM IS _____

That's because _____
_____
_____

## THE MOST EXCITING WWE SUPERSTAR IS _____

That's because _____
_____
_____

## THE MOST HARDWORKING WWE SUPERSTAR IS _____

That's because _____
_____
_____

## THE MOST LOYAL WWE SUPERSTAR IS _____

That's because _____
_____
_____

## THE MOST EXCITING WWE SUPERSTAR IS _____

That's because _____
_____
_____

## THE FUNNIEST WWE SUPERSTAR IS _____

That's because _____
_____
_____

## THE MOST HONEST WWE SUPERSTAR IS _____

That's because _____
_____
_____

# JOKIN' AROUND

WWE Superstars love to unwind with a good joke. The more of these you know when you head into the locker room, the better! Here are some hilarious hits to get you started. . . .

**Q:** Why did Seth Rollins go to bed with measuring tape under his pillow?

**A:** He wanted to see how long he could sleep!

**Q:** What kind of keys does Otis love most?

**A:** Cookies!

**Q:** What can WWE Superstars hold without using their hands?

**A:** Their breath!

**Q:** What kind of flower grows under Mandy Rose's nose?

**A:** Tulips!

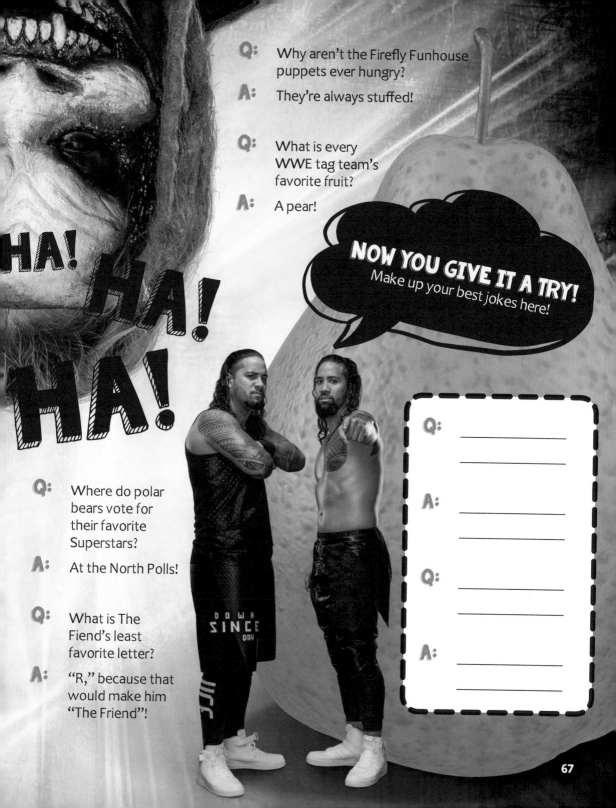

**Q:** Why aren't the Firefly Funhouse puppets ever hungry?

**A:** They're always stuffed!

**Q:** What is every WWE tag team's favorite fruit?

**A:** A pear!

**NOW YOU GIVE IT A TRY!**
Make up your best jokes here!

HA! HA! HA! HA!

**Q:** Where do polar bears vote for their favorite Superstars?

**A:** At the North Polls!

**Q:** What is The Fiend's least favorite letter?

**A:** "R," because that would make him "The Friend"!

**Q:** _____
_____

**A:** _____
_____

**Q:** _____
_____

**A:** _____
_____

# TRAVEL TIME!

Did you know that WWE Superstars travel all over the world almost every day of the year? If you got the chance to visit these amazing countries, what would you like to do, see, and learn?

If I went to Japan, I would . . .

_____

_____

One thing I know about Japan is . . .

_____

_____

One thing I'd like to learn about Japan is . . .

_____

_____

## 2)

If I went to Ireland, I would . . .

_____

_____


One thing I know about Ireland is . . .

_____

_____


One thing I'd like to learn about Ireland is . . .

_____

_____


## 3)

If I went to Mexico, I would . . .

_____

_____


One thing I know about Mexico is . . .

_____

_____


One thing I'd like to learn about Mexico is . . .

_____

_____

# PACK YOUR SUPERSTAR SUITCASE!

Traveling like a WWE Superstar is hard work! Think about what to put in your luggage to make your time on the road more fun. Write up a list below and then draw it in the open suitcase! (Try not to overpack!)

# MASTER THE MIC!

Fill in the blanks to create a crowd-pleasing speech and unlock your inner Superstar, then cut out the microphone on the opposite page and practice your speech over and over. (If your family gets annoyed, try practicing in front of your cat instead!)

"LISTEN HERE, _____ (NAME OF YOUR OPPONENT). I KNOW I'M NOT THE MOST _____ (ADJECTIVE) SUPERSTAR IN WWE, BUT I KNOW I CAN _____ (VERB) BETTER THAN ANY _____ (NOUN) OUT THERE. AND IF YOU THINK YOU'RE GOING TO COME INTO MY RING WITH YOUR _____ (ADJECTIVE) _____ (NOUN) AND START _____ (VERB)ING ME AND ALL OF MY FANS, YOU'RE MORE _____ (ADJECTIVE) THAN A _____ (NOUN) COVERED IN _____ (PLURAL NOUN). I'M READY TO COMPETE, I'M READY TO WIN, AND I'M READY TO _____ (VERB). AND NOTHING IS GOING TO STAND IN MY WAY—NOT EVEN A(N) _____ (ADJECTIVE) _____ (NOUN) LIKE YOU!"

**STEP 1:** Decorate your mic WWE-style!

**STEP 2:** Cut it out along the solid lines.

**STEP 3:** Fold the dotted lines and add tape to secure everything in place.

**STEP 4:** "Check! Check! Is this thing on?"

# SHOWSTOPPERS!

How well do you know the names of **WWE**'s biggest events and shows? Hopefully you can help whoever runs the Titan Tron unscramble them before the boss finds out what happened!

**1) LAWNIESTMARE**

This is _____

**2) ARLESMUMMS**

This is _____

**3) REBURYMOALL**

This is _____

**4) SOSEIRSURVIVER**

This is _____

**5) ELLCLANELHI**

This is _____

**6) BETHINKYONMEAN**

This is _____

Answer key on pages 93–95

# SUPERSTAR SEARCH

If you're going to rule the ring, you'll need to know the names of everyone in your way. Look at the list of names below and find them in the word search. Answers can be across, up and down, backward, and diagonal!

```
M D M U I Z S M K S L E I M P P N C E T
K W C W N T I J I Q E O A T C U E J E R
M G E R Y T N I C M W E R D Y R O U M S
S M S O A R E O T E U H E O A I P N E Y
J O H N C E N A N A R M I I C E Y L U A
B R A U N S T R O W M A N S D J E A T O
U I J C E Y D A J S T Y L E S E L C E D
B T H A A R O M A N R E I G N S Y E H A
E I U I Y Y N O T R O Y D N A R A Y C N
C N P E R E A X K V T D S T T L B E O I
K P R K F M N L S T E B N E C M X V C E
Y S E T H R O L L I N S Z E L V I A I L
L U N D E R T A K E R O S J I I B N R B
Y U A A N C A U H C R E N I G F A S O R
N U D E G D E C J M S A B X T R E S L Y
C X R P P A L E X A B L I S S O E H Q A
H E T S K N A B A H S A S W A K U S A N
```

ALEXA BLISS    EDGE    THE FIEND
SETH ROLLINS    BECKY LYNCH
AJ STYLES    DREW MCINTYRE    ROMAN REIGNS
JOHN CENA    BRAUN STROWMAN    LACEY EVANS    SASHA BANKS
RANDY ORTON    UNDERTAKER    DANIEL BRYAN
ASUKA    BAYLEY    ELIAS    OTIS    RICOCHET

Answer key on pages 93–95

# DESIGN YOUR TOUR BUS!

Did you know that some WWE Superstars travel on their very own buses? And they're waaaaay cooler than school buses. Decorate yours so that your fans will know whenever you come to town.

# DECK OUT YOUR DRESSING ROOM!

If you thought decorating your bedroom was cool, wait until you decorate your very own dressing room! As a top WWE Superstar, what do you need in here to prepare for your next match? (And what will you want just because it's awesome?)

# NAME YOUR FINISHER!

Still need a name for your fearsome finisher? Have no fear! Just take the first letters of your first and last names and consult the corresponding lists. What'd you come up with?

## FIRST LETTER OF YOUR FIRST NAME

**A** – Mega

**B** – Amazing

**C** – Wonderful

**D** – Scary

**E** – Thunderous

**F** – Gorgeous

**G** – Thrilling

**H** – Devastating

**I** – Mind-blowing

**J** – Deafening

**K** – Original

**L** – Cunning

**M** – Elegant

**N** – First-class

**O** – Energetic

**P** – Astonishing

**Q** – Magnificent

**R** – Horrible

**S** – Stinky

**T** – Stunning

**U** – Shocking

**V** – Dreadful

**W** – Breathtaking

**X** – Heart-stopping

**Y** – Exciting

**Z** – Impressive

# FIRST LETTER OF YOUR LAST NAME

A – Cheese
B – Lightning
C – Hippopotamus
D – Snorkel
E – Elevator
F – Bolt
G – Cardigan
H – Sandwich
I – Kitty
J – Pickle
K – Spider
L – Selfie
M – Couch

N – Laser
O – Toilet
P – Unicycle
Q – Moose
R – Casaba Melon
S – Buzzer
T – Goblin
U – Destroyer
V – Tank
W – Armadillo
X – Teddy Bear
Y – Backpack
Z – Mustache

## MY FINISHER IS CALLED

THE _____

# A DAY IN THE LIFE OF A NEW SUPERSTAR

In order to keep up with your Superstar responsibilities, you'll need to set a tight schedule! Imagine what you'll be doing from the moment you wake up until the moment you go to sleep. Don't forget to eat, rest, and relax, either!

| TIME | EVENT |
| --- | --- |
| 7:00 AM – 8:00 AM | |
| 8:00 AM – 10:00 AM | |
| 10:00 AM – 10:30 AM | |
| 10:30 AM – 12:00 PM | |
| 12:00 PM – 1:30 PM | |
| 1:30 PM – 2:30 PM | |
| 2:30 PM – 3:30 PM | |
| 3:30 PM – 4:00 PM | |
| 4:00 PM – 5:00 PM | |
| 5:00 PM – 6:30 PM | |
| 6:30 PM – 10:00 PM | |

# CHAMPIONSHIP CROSSWORD PUZZLE

Use the clues to show how much you know about your fellow WWE Superstars.

## ACROSS

3    WWE's Friday Night Show

5    I once called myself The Architect

7    I'm known as The Phenom

8    I earned the WWE Championship at *WrestleMania* 36

12    I'm rarely seen without my guitar

14    This is where *WrestleMania* 36 was held

15    Undertaker buried me alive during the Boneyard Match

## DOWN

1    This is where Bray Wyatt plays with his puppet friends

2    The New Day is comprised of Kofi Kingston, Big E, and . . .

4    Where future WWE Superstars start their journey

6    Randy Orton uses me as a finisher (I'm also his initials!)

9    I made my surprise comeback at the 2020 Royal Rumble

10    My finisher is known as The Bank Statement

11    My finisher is the 630 Senton

13    Winner of the first WWE Women's Royal Rumble

Answer key on pages 93–95

# ROAD TO WRESTLEMANIA BOARD GAME

Your journey to *WrestleMania* won't be easy. But it will be fun! Grab some future Superstar friends and see who can make his or her way to The Grandest Stage of Them All first!

## WHAT YOU NEED:

- Dice
- A group of friends
- Avatars (like coins or WWE action figures)

## RULES:

1. Determine who goes first by having each player roll the dice. The highest number goes first, the second-highest second, and so on.

2. The game starts on square one. Roll the dice before each turn, and then move your avatar forward the correct number of squares.

3. If you land on a square at the bottom of a ladder, climb to the top of it. If you land on a square at the top, nothing happens.

4. If you land on a square at the top of a rope, slide down to the bottom. If you land on a square at the bottom, nothing happens.

5. The first player to reach square 48 wins!

| 48 | 47 You were forced to tap out! | 46 | 45 | 44 | 43 |
|---|---|---|---|---|---|
| 37 | 38 | 39 | 40 You drew #30 in the Royal Rumble! | 41 | 42 You lost your match on *Raw*! |
| 36 | 35 | 34 Handicap Match: you vs. Randy Orton and A.J. Styles! | 33 | 32 | 31 |
| 25 You just won the Intercontinental Championship! | 26 | 27 | 28 | 29 | 30 |
| 24 | 23 | 22 You got eliminated from the Royal Rumble! | 21 | 20 | 19 |
| 13 | 14 | 15 | 16 | 17 | 18 You got lost in the Firefly Funhouse! |
| 12 | 11 | 10 | 9 | 8 | 7 |
| 1 | 2 The crowd loves you! | 3 | 4 | 5 Braun Strowman wants to be your tag team partner! | 6 |

# POWER PROFILE

Fill in everything so we can break down your strengths, weaknesses, and accomplishments as a future WWE Superstar!

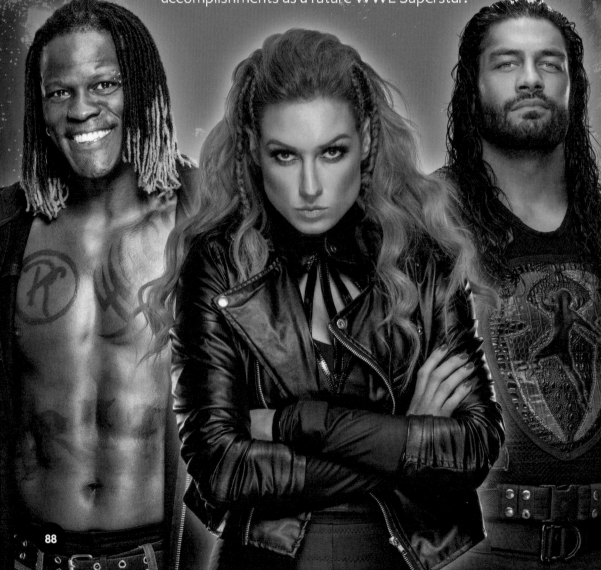

Height: _____

Weight: _____

Hometown: _____

Birthday: _____ / _____ / _____

List three of your strengths:

1. _____

2. _____

3. _____

List three of your weaknesses:

1. _____

2. _____

3. _____

List your three dream opponents:

1. _____

2. _____

3. _____

On a scale from 1–10, where do you rank in these Superstar attributes?

| | | | | | | | | | | |
|---|---|---|---|---|---|---|---|---|---|---|
| Strength | 1 | 2 | 3 | 4 | 5 | 6 | 7 | 8 | 9 | 10 |
| Speed | 1 | 2 | 3 | 4 | 5 | 6 | 7 | 8 | 9 | 10 |
| Courage | 1 | 2 | 3 | 4 | 5 | 6 | 7 | 8 | 9 | 10 |
| Honesty | 1 | 2 | 3 | 4 | 5 | 6 | 7 | 8 | 9 | 10 |
| Creativity | 1 | 2 | 3 | 4 | 5 | 6 | 7 | 8 | 9 | 10 |

# WWE SUPERSTAR
## APPLICATION

It's time to tell everyone in WWE just what a great future Superstar you'll be. Answer these questions which will help WWE get to know the real you!

1)   **WHAT IS YOUR PROUDEST ACCOMPLISHMENT?**

_____

2)   **WHAT WOULD YOU DO IF YOU WERE LOCKED IN A ROOM WITH THE FIEND?**

_____

3)   **IF ANOTHER WWE SUPERSTAR WANTED YOU TO CHEAT TO WIN A MATCH, WHAT WOULD YOU DO?**

_____

4)   **HOW WOULD YOU HELP A FELLOW WWE SUPERSTAR WHO WAS HAVING TROUBLE SUCCEEDING?**

_____

5)   **WHICH WWE SUPERSTAR WOULD YOU TURN TO FOR ADVICE?**

_____   _____

6)   **WHAT WILL MAKE YOU THE BEST WWE SUPERSTAR OF ALL TIME?**

_____

_____

# LETTER TO THE BOSS

Now's your chance to tell Triple H—COO of WWE—why you deserve to be a WWE Superstar. Think it over, and don't be shy!

**DEAR TRIPLE H,**

# YOUR WWE SUPERSTAR CONTRACT!

Congratulations! You did it! You made it! You're a **WWE** Superstar! All that's left to do is sign on the dotted line below. After you've named your terms, of course.

I, _____ , accept **WWE**'s offer to make me the next **WWE** Superstar! As a WWE Superstar, I promise that I will always act honorably, tell the truth, be brave, and offer help to those in need. I also promise that I will do my best in every situation, no matter how scary or challenging it may be. I will be nice and kind to my fellow Superstars, as well as my friends, family, animals, and other people who I meet. In doing these things, I will always continue to represent **WWE** as the most awesome Superstar I can be!

Signed:                                              Signed:

P.S. I also get to eat ice cream whenever I want and will require one fire-breathing dragon to ride to the ring.

# ANSWER KEY

## P 14 YOU'RE A-MAZE-ING!

## P 19 WAIT A MINUTE . . .

## P 25 SUPERSTAR FACE-OFF!

A) Alexa Bliss

B) Braun Strowman

C) The Fiend

D) Charlotte Flair

E) Kevin Owens

F) Nia Jax

G) Sasha Banks

H) Otis

I) Baron Corbin

1) The Rock

2) Moonsault

3) Roman Reigns

4) Turnbuckle

5) NXT

# P 40 THE ULTIMATE FUTURE WWE SUPERSTAR QUIZ!

1) d      4) b      7) d
2) c      5) a      8) b
3) c      6) b      9) c

# P 42 CHAMPIONSHIP CHASE!

# P 48 SUPERSTAR EYE SPY!

 F.     H.     D.     L.     K.    A.

 C.     E.     B.     G.     J.     I.

## P 56 SCRAMBLED SUPERSTARS

1) A.J. Styles
2) Bobby Lashley
3) Dolph Ziggler
4) Otis
5) Seth Rollins
6) Charlotte
7) Randy Orton
8) Ruby Riott
9) Roman Reigns
10) Drew McIntyre

## P 63 LEGEND LOOKOUT

1) Hulk Hogan
2) Macho Man
3) Ultimate Warrior
4) Shawn Michaels
5) The Rock
6) Stone Cold Steve Austin

## P 75 SHOWSTOPPERS!

1) WrestleMania
2) SummerSlam
3) Royal Rumble
4) Survivor Series
5) Hell in a Cell
6) Money in the Bank

## P 76 SUPERSTAR SEARCH

```
M D M U I Z S M K S A S H A B A N K S T
K W C W N T I J I Q E O A T C U E J E R
M G E R Y T N I C M W E R D Y R O U M S
S M S O A R E O T E U H E O A I P N E Y
J O H N C E N A N A R M I I C E Y L U A
B R A U N S T R O W M A N S D J E A T O
U I J C E Y D A J S T Y L E S E L C E D
B T H A A R O M A N R E I G N S Y E H A
E I U I Y Y N O T R O Y D N A R A Y C N
C N P T H E F I E N D D S T T L B E O I
K P R K F M N L S T E B N E C M X V C E
Y S E T H R O L L I N S Z E L V I A I L
L U N D E R T A K E R O S J I I B N R B
Y U A A N C A U H C R E N I G F A S O R
N U D E G D E C J M S A B X T R E S L Y
C X R P P A L E X A B L I S S O E H Q A
H E T S K N A B A H S A S W A K U S A N
```

## P 84 CHAMPIONSHIP CROSSWORD PUZZLE

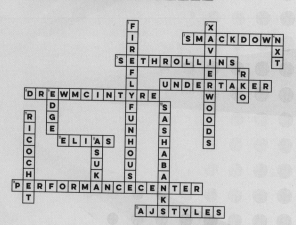

# YOUR VERY FIRST AUTOGRAPH

As the newest WWE Superstar, would you do us the honor of signing your very first autograph right here? Take this book wherever you go, and maybe you can add some other Superstars' signatures as well!